when someone you love has

*A*lzheimer's

SELECTED BOOKS BY EARL A. GROLLMAN

Bereaved Children and Teens: A Support Guide for Parents and Professionals (editor)

Caring and Coping When Your Loved One Is Seriously Ill

Caring for Your Aged Parents (with Sharon Hya Grollman)

Concerning Death: A Practical Guide for the Living (editor)

Explaining Divorce to Children (editor)

In Sickness and in Health: How to Cope When Your Loved One Is Ill

Living When a Loved One Has Died

Straight Talk about Death for Teenagers: How to Cope with Losing Someone You Love

Suicide: Prevention, Intervention, Postvention

Talking about Death: A Dialogue between Parent and Child

Time Remembered: A Journal for Survivors

What Helped Me When My Loved One Died (editor)

When Someone You Love Has Alzheimer's: The Caregiver's Journey (with Kenneth S. Kosik, M.D.)

When Your Loved One Is Dying

BOOKS BY KENNETH S. KOSIK, M.D.

When Someone You Love Has Alzheimer's: The Caregiver's Journey (with Earl A. Grollman)

EARL A. GROLLMAN
AND KENNETH S. KOSIK, M.D.

when someone you love has

Alzheimer's

the Caregiver's Journey

BEACON PRESS
BOSTON

Beacon Press
25 Beacon Street
Boston, Massachusetts 02108-2892

Beacon Press books
are published under the auspices of
the Unitarian Universalist Association of Congregations.

01 00 99 98 97   8 7 6 5 4 3 2

Text design by Jeannet Leendertse
Composition by Electronic Publishing Services, Inc.

Library of Congress Cataloging-in-Publication Data can be found on page 164.

"Reflections of an Alzheimer's Caregiver" by Cy Moffit reprinted by permission
of the author.

The recommendations and information in this book are not a substitute for
medical diagnosis. For specific information concerning your personal medical
condition, consult a physician.

To Netta: The Consummate Caregiver,
Always with Love

> *To Sally, Abe, Leah, Miyoung, Russell,*
> *Sabrina, and Eena*

ℛℯ

contents

Acknowledgments

The vision and encouragement of our editor Susan Worst are incalculable in the creation of our book. A warm and heartfelt thank-you to Elly Schottman for her continual support and keen insights. We are so grateful to Eileen Salmanson and Stephanie Brett for their advice and criticisms as well as Leah Rochbert, Stephen Hoffman, Dorothy Stoneman, and Jane Salk for their personal stories and practical ideas. Kathy Mann-Koepke was of enormous help in compiling the Resources section. We are in debt to her and to the Washington University Alzheimer Center for their comments on the material suggested in Further Reading.

Most of all, particular mention must be given to the countless caregivers who shared with us their journey—their anguish, dreams, and blueprints for living in the face of a loved one's Alzheimer's disease. It is our fervent hope that a cure may be forthcoming and that this book will become obsolete.

⤢

Introduction

The part of life we live as elders is a gift. Very few species live as long beyond the reproductive years as humans do. Perhaps we have this relatively long life span because elders serve such important roles in human society: as repositories of wisdom, keepers of history and family memories, and backup caregivers for the young. The feeling of joy that comes from filling these roles—the joy of grandchildren, the joy of allowing others to benefit from our experience—is built into the design of human life.

Lives that conclude without that final chapter, without the time to grow old and gain perspective, often seem bitterly incomplete. But the greatest loss, the greatest dehumanization, is to grow old without possession of your mind. That is Alzheimer's disease.

Alzheimer's disease affects an estimated four million Americans. Studies indicate that ten percent of the population aged 65 and over suffers from the disease. The incidence of Alzheimer's increases with age. Twenty percent of individuals aged seventy-five to eighty-four, and nearly half of all people eighty-five and older, are afflicted. No race, gender, or socioeconomic class is exempt from this disease.

Former President Ronald Reagan demonstrated great courage when he revealed that he had been stricken with Alzheimer's disease. He called it "a journey that will lead me to the sunset of my life." Despite this image, Alzheimer's disease is not a pleasant twilight stroll. It is a progressive brain disorder, fatal, but slow. Patients often linger through years of increasing decline and dependency.

Alzheimer's disease has a devastating effect not only on the patient, but also on family and friends. Almost seventy percent of Alzheimer's patients in this country are cared for at home. For the caregiver, the responsibility and grief can seem endless. Those who have loved and cared for Alzheimer's patients have called this period in their life "an ongoing funeral" and "the thirty-six-hour day." To watch helplessly as a loved one is transformed into an Alzheimer's patient is a horrible, heartbreaking experience. Yet, through the sorrow and exhaustion, you may experience positive emotions and understanding. You may also find patience, tolerance, forgiveness, humor, compassion, and an ever-expanding capacity to shift priorities. Above all, you will know love.

It is a difficult and sobering task to have to accept the tragedy of Alzheimer's in your life and then face the future with courage and resourcefulness. We hope that this book will help you better understand the disease and the needs of your loved one as well as your own emotions and assist you in finding ways to honor and meet your own needs.

For the Alzheimer's caregiver, the journey is long and rough, its path winding and arduous. There are no correct solutions to the challenges you face. This book is not a trail guide. Each caregiver must make decisions based on his or her needs and circumstances, and the needs of their loved ones. We hope that the information and support offered in this book will help you face each new challenge and decision with courage and compassion for all involved.

ACCEPTING THE DIAGNOSIS, GRIEVING THE LOSS

Alzheimer's disease.

There's no way to cushion the news,
no way to soften the blow.

Your loved one has a devastating disease
that will radically change both of your lives.

Inside you may feel a scream of anguish, NO!
as your whole being rejects the words being spoken.

Or you may feel numb, in a trance,
a strange frozen calmness,
as if the doctor must be addressing someone else.
Not you.

You may experience a sad sense of confirmation.

"Of course," you may think.
"That explains so much.
His erratic behavior,
the arguments,
the sense that he hasn't been himself,
that something is terribly wrong."

To live with Alzheimer's disease.

For those afflicted and those who love them,
it is a journey of grief.
You grieve for your beloved, as well as for yourself.

Grief is the process through which
love says good-bye.

Grieving for an Alzheimer's patient is heart-rending
in a unique and terrible way.

It is the ongoing mourning
of a person who in many ways is no longer here,
but whose body lingers on.

The daughter and caregiver of an Alzheimer's victim
    explains,

"My father was a shell of himself.
The man that he had been, my father whom I had loved and
    who had loved me,
was not there.
I grieved for my father and missed him terribly,
long before he was physically gone,
and afterward as well."

Alzheimer's disease destroys the mind,
eroding and gradually destroying the qualities of the person
    you love.

You mourn the loss of your adventuresome partner,
your competent, energetic parent,
your fun-loving friend.

Your loved one is replaced by
a patient who may no longer recognize you,
who may be suspicious, irritable, aggressive.

As caretaker of an Alzheimer's patient,
you do not have the luxury of abandoning yourself to grief.
You must grieve as you struggle to meet
the new responsibilities and challenges
that present themselves each day.

Shock, denial, panic, guilt, anger, depression, bodily distress.

These emotions are not neat, sequential stages
leading you through the process of grief.
They are recurring themes of anguish as you confront an
    unfair fate.
At different times, different emotions will predominate.

Learning about the various facets of grief may help you
accept your own barrage of feelings
as you journey through this sad and difficult time.

Remember, there is no right way or wrong way to grieve,
no prescribed time it will take you to adjust.
Each person experiences grief in his or her own way.

Step by step, day by day,
you find your way through.

Shock

The test results leave little doubt.
Your loved one has Alzheimer's disease.
When you learn the bad news, numbness may insulate you
from the enormity of the pain.

It is a protective mechanism,
allowing the grimness of the reality
to seep in gradually.

The shock may not wear off until hours,
or days,
after the doctor's pronouncement.

Women's Health Services
CABELL HUNTINGTON HOSPITAL

1/9/04

Dear Roberta,

Without your and Jessie's support and love during these past 7 years, I could NOT have walked this journey. Now, as you begin your journey down this sometimes scary path, please know that I and others love you & will help For More Information Phone in any way 304 / 526-2270 we can.

Love, Patricia

Then intolerable feelings may crash upon you,
sweeping you into
a crushing undertow of despair,

"It can't be!
Not my loved one. Not us."

Allow yourself time and space for adjustment.

You are a person of courage and inner resources.
You have met challenges before in your life.

Somehow, you will find the strength
to do what you can,
as best you can.

One day at a time;
one step at a time.

Denial

To accept your loved one's diagnosis may seem unthinkable.
How can you accept losing your loved one this way?

"It can't be true!
There must be another explanation,
a way to fix the problem,
a way to save my loved one
and myself."

Denial is a coping tool,
a part of grief.
When life seems unbearable,
denial intervenes.

Denial
is nature's way of
buffering an awful blow,
distancing us from the pain,
giving us time to absorb the facts,
and accept the truth.

Denial can give us
time and space
to gather the strength
and courage we need
to face the pain of losing our loved one
to a terrible disease.

As the disease progresses,
there are good days and bad days.
Sometimes your loved one may seem much better,
almost like the person you once knew.
Hope and denial may spring up again.

"Maybe my loved one is getting better!"

When bad days return,
reality returns.

Tragically, at this point in time,
Alzheimer's disease is fatal.
There is no known cure.
As the disease progresses,
the patient's condition steadily declines.

In order to make plans for appropriate care,
you must be able to move beyond denial
and face the facts of the disease.

Pretending that nothing is wrong
after the initial shock has passed
can prevent you from
seeking the help and protection
the patient may need,
particularly if he or she lives alone.

In order to plan for the future,
you must have the courage
to accept the sorrowful truth.

Some thoughts:
If your loved one is in the early stages of the disease
there is probably still time
to fulfill some dreams and goals.
Alzheimer's disease does not cripple a person overnight.

Share the pleasures that still bring you both delight.
Go on long walks together.
Listen to music.
Enjoy the garden.
Get together with small groups of close friends
and family members.
Strengthen bonds with those you love.

Because sudden change can be disorienting and upsetting
to many Alzheimer's patients,
it is best to stay close to the familiar.

Begin to explore local resources for yourself and your loved
one:
Alzheimer's organizations, day care programs, home
services.
Begin to build a community of support
for the difficult journey that lies ahead.

Panic

When the veils of shock and denial lift,
when your understanding of Alzheimer's disease is
    deepened,
you may find yourself
clutched
by panic.

"Will she forget who I am?"
"Will he wander away and get lost?"
"How can I take care of him?"
"What about the rest of my family? What about my job?"
"Who's going to pay for all this?"

Panic makes your chest grow tight,
constricts your throat,
knots your stomach.

Driving familiar routes, you suddenly become disoriented.
Sounds in the house at night become eerie and frightening.
In the midst of an errand, you forget what you were doing.

You dream of being smothered,
lost,
falling,
knowing there is no one to help you.

You try to organize the problem into manageable
    dimensions,
try to lay plans for disaster control.
But you feel yourself flailing,
becoming paralyzed, incapable of effective action.

"I just want to run away!"

People can tolerate almost anything
as long as they have some hope
that things will get better.
With Alzheimer's, can there be hope?

You are overloaded
emotionally, spiritually, intellectually.
You need time to collect yourself
and draw on your inner strength.

Accept that you do not have the power
to control the disease or make it go away,
but know also that there are still some things
you can do:
      care for your loved one,
      show kindness and affection,
      celebrate small achievements.

Guilt

It's too late.
"I should have spent more time with my loved one before,
done the things I promised,
taken the trips we always planned."

Is Alzheimer's disease the punishment for not taking the
    time
to appreciate the one you loved most?

Now, you feel trapped.

There are other reasons to feel guilty.

Perhaps you are embarrassed
at your loved one's condition and actions.

You may be avoiding social events—
church, temple, even family gatherings—
wanting to preserve your loved one's dignity,
wanting to protect yourself
from public humiliation.

"I know it's not her fault.
It's the disease.
But still I feel so angry and impatient.
And so guilty for feeling that way."

Guilt and anger may plague you throughout the duration
of your loved one's disease.

At times you may wish
the body
that used to house your loved one
and is now occupied by a disease
would cease to function,
would die,
releasing your loved one
from the indignities of the disease
and liberating you from the burden of
witnessing this awful transformation.

Then you may feel pangs of remorse,
as if wishing something to be
might make it so.

From time to time you may lose your temper and lash out
at the patient.
Afterward you may feel riddled with guilt.

At times, you will choose to ignore your loved one's
nonsensical demands,
while inside you seethe with anger.
Afterward you may chastise yourself
for your lack of feeling and compassion.

Maybe you will decide to remove yourself from the role of
primary caretaker, explaining, "It's just too painful."
Afterward you may agonize over the decision.
Have you abandoned and betrayed your loved one?

Guilt and sorrow.

"It never goes away," confides a caregiver.
"The feeling that there's more I should be doing . . .
that there's nothing I can do."

So much guilt
for things said or thought or done.

So many regrets
for something you should have said or done.

If you had known that your loved one would contract
    Alzheimer's disease,
you might have acted and done things differently.
If you could undo yesterday's angry words and actions,
you would.

All of us let loving feelings go unexpressed.
All of us fail people who care about us.

Accept your fallibility.
You're only human. Your resources are limited.
Treat yourself with compassion.
Forgive.

When you berate yourself,
you sap yourself
of needed energy.

Forgive.

And move on to tomorrow.

Anger

As months pass and memory fails,
the person you love is gradually being transformed
into a patient.
Someone for whom you feel compassion and care
and yet regard with a certain remoteness.
Is this patient still your loved one?
Or has your loved one already departed, leaving only the
    shell behind?

As you endure
the embarrassing behaviors,
the groundless suspicions,
the same questions asked over and over and over,
your sense of helplessness and mourning
may turn to overwhelming rage.

"Why me?
Why my spouse, lover, sibling, parent, friend?
What did we do to deserve this?"

You feel fury toward God
for being unjust and capricious.

Fury toward your loved one
whose illness has plunged you both into this hell.

Fury toward the doctors and nurses
for not doing more, for not trying harder.
Where are the wonder drugs?
The marvels of modern medicine?

Fury against your own inability to help your loved one,
to solve the problem.

Fury toward your family and friends
for their unreasonable suggestions and
their criticism of the way you are handling the situation.
Fury at their failure to appreciate the enormity of your task.

Fury toward yourself for succumbing to rage.

But rage helps you release your anguish and frustration
at an intolerable situation.

Anger is a feeling,
a part of grief.

It doesn't have to be right.

It doesn't have to make sense.

You need to acknowledge, express, and resolve these painful
    feelings.
Holding back your anger too much
can lead to deep self-destructive depression.

Understand the real reasons for your hostility.
Anger may be a more comfortable and empowering
response to a dreadful situation
than vulnerability and fear.

Distinguish between current anger
and old unresolved anger.

Know that anger and revenge are not the same.

Find constructive ways to release your rage so that
your fury does not become a curse,
so that your anger does not cost you too dearly
in terms of inner stress,
fractured relationships,
and your own health and strength.

When your anger wells up against your loved one,
remember that he or she has no control over the irritating
    actions.
You are both victims of a cruel, debilitating disease.
Direct your anger at the disease.

It is inevitable that sometimes you will yell or snap at the
    patient.
It is a warning sign that your frustration level is getting
    high.
Try to take some time off and renew your patience.

If you find yourself striking or shaking the patient in anger,
the situation has become serious.
You must seek help.
Work with family, friends, and professional counselors
to find ways
to alter the caregiving arrangements
to reduce stress and resentment.

Find ways to release your fury:

- 🙵   Talk it out with a friend or counselor.

- 🙵   Write an angry letter with accusations and threats, then seal it up so no one will read it.

- 🙵   Take a long walk.

- 🙵   Go outside and scream.

- 🙵   Meditate, practice relaxation techniques.

- 🙵   Tear up an old phone book.

- 🙵   Race around until you are tired.

- 🙵   Beat on a mattress.

- 🙵   Listen to music.

- 🙵   Try to forgive yourself and others.

Depression

Plummeted to rock bottom,
you feel worthless, incapable, inadequate.
Simple tasks are intimidating.
Your lack of concentration is causing your life to derail.
"I forgot we had an appointment; I was so preoccupied."

Self-pity and despair engulf you.
Is life still worth living?
If only you could curl up in bed and never open your eyes
    again.

Like denial and shock,
depression is a way of shutting down the emotional system
in response to overload.

You have every reason to experience depression.
Your depression is part of mourning
the slow excruciating death of someone you love,
a person who is no longer fully with you,
though the body lingers on.

As you are pulled down in an emotional spiral of
    depression,
you resent people's gestures of encouragement and help.

Depression has been defined as "anger turned inward."

You're no longer able to experience pleasure.
You get upset easily and cry over "little things."
You have difficulty concentrating, remembering,
making decisions.
You neglect your appearance; you have no interest in
personal care.

"Leave me alone."
"I don't care anymore."

The term *depression* is also used to describe a serious
   medical condition.

How do you know if the depression you are experiencing
is a normal and appropriate grief response,
or if it has escalated into a clinical disease?

The distinction is mostly a matter of intensity and duration.
Here are a few indicators that may be helpful.

Do you feel angry as well as depressed? If so, that's a good
   sign.
A clinically depressed person does not usually have the
   energy
to feel or acknowledge anger.

Can you still, at times, find comfort
in the support of friends and the things that used to bring
   you pleasure?
That responsiveness is a good sign of mental health and
   resilience.

If . . .

- you have concerns about your mental well-being,

- you feel your depression has lasted too long,

- you find yourself sinking deeper and deeper into apathy,

- you feel overwhelmed with feelings of worthlessness and despair, and

- nothing you do seems to relieve these symptoms,

do not hesitate to consult a therapist, psychiatrist, or psychologist.

If you are clinically depressed, there are ways to remedy the condition.
A caring and knowledgeable adviser can help you negotiate your way through these difficult times.

To acknowledge our problems and seek help is often the most courageous and responsible act any of us can take.

Bodily Distress

"I can't remember the last time I felt good."

Inside your chest lives a heavy jagged pain.
Your head throbs,
your stomach aches,
your mouth feels dry.
You break out in strange rashes.
Exhaustion and lack of concentration
make it impossible to complete necessary tasks.

You begin to worry that you too
are starting to experience the symptoms of Alzheimer's.

These physical problems are real.
You are not a hypochondriac.

Your body is responding to the strain of bereavement.
Stress weakens your resistance to disease,
aggravating former medical conditions,
creating new problems.

An aching heart
takes a physical toll on the rest of your body.

Especially at this time, you need to take care of yourself.
Consult an understanding physician.
Be sure that you mention that your loved one has
     Alzheimer's disease.

As you work through your grief,
your symptoms may begin to diminish.

chapter
2

BEGINNING TO COPE

Until a cure is found,
the progression of Alzheimer's disease is inevitable.
Your loved one is no longer the same person as before.

Your pain is a reminder that both of your lives are changing.

Caring for an Alzheimer's patient is an exhausting
and sometimes frightening task.

So much is outside your control.

Because different patients are afflicted
with different symptoms
to varying degrees,
there is no way to predict the course of the illness.
There is no way to "be prepared."
The only thing you can do is to
deal with each symptom that occurs, as it occurs.

A Chinese proverb says,
"The journey of a thousand miles
starts with a single step."

Perhaps the first step of your journey
as a caregiver
is to accept the limits of your power
to influence the course of events
and protect your loved one.

No matter how slow you say things,
how many times you explain them,
how many times you show them,
it may not help.

The truth is that you cannot control
the disease that is ravaging your loved one
and causing dreadful changes in both of your lives.

You can only choose how you will meet
the challenges of the ordeal.

Letting go of the need to be in control
may lessen the burden and help you
accept the reality of the disease.

You are beginning your trek
down a long path of dilemmas,
temporary solutions,
and more dilemmas.

There are probably no solutions that will
satisfy everyone involved.

You can, however, earnestly try to make the best decision
at each juncture,
knowing that as the disease progresses,
circumstances will change,
and you will need to seek new solutions.

"If there is a sin against life,
it consists not so much as
despairing of life
rather than in hoping for another."
— *Albert Camus*

Taking care of yourself

Your loved one's condition may change from moment to
     moment.
Communication with your loved one, family, and health
     care professionals
will be difficult at times.

As a caregiver, you must continually
seek answers for yourself and your loved one.
It is a long and painful process.

Caregiving is a high-stress activity.

You will often be exhausted, emotionally drained.

It is imperative that you acknowledge and respect your own
    needs.
Heed the voice of the child inside you,
"I'm important too!"
and respond with kindness and understanding.

Don't become a martyr.
If you are consumed by your loved one's needs,
you neglect yourself and other significant people.

When you fuse your own identity with your loved one,
you lose your own identity.

You are more than a caregiver.
You are yourself.

Acknowledge the long struggle ahead.
Acknowledge the difficulties of the struggle.

If you collapse under the strain,
you will not be as effective as you would like
in supporting the one who needs you.

Find an equilibrium of giving to yourself and giving to
others.

*"If I am not for myself,
who is?"*

— *Rabbi Hillel*

Quiet times

You cannot devote
every minute of every day
to vigilant watchfulness over
the loved one who has become your patient.

You must have a respite
from emotionally draining demands.

Make it a priority to counteract the stress of caregiving,
so that anxiety and terror will not overpower you.

You need interludes of rest and separation—
physical, emotional, and spiritual.
Not to abandon your loved one, but to find a balance
between caring for others and attending to your own needs.

The demands of caregiving
can leave you feeling very much alone and deserted.
It is important that you seek companionship
and renew and affirm aspects of your life
that can nurture you.
Make arrangements to meet friends regularly for lunch, a
    walk, a movie.

Leave spaces in each day
for meditation, prayer,
or quiet moments just for yourself.
Rediscover the healing aspects of solitude.

Slow down.
Relinquish responsibility.
Turn within for a measure of peace and quiet.

Take a one-hour vacation.
Spend a little time in a quiet place,
  a lovely green park
  a museum
  an empty church, synagogue, or mosque.

Go for a walk.
Take note of the nature that surrounds you.

Close your eyes, relax, and listen to music.
Let the surge of sound transport you to another world.

The peace that you find
will make you a better caregiver.

"When from our better selves we have too long
Been parted by the hurrying world, and droop
. . . .
How gracious, how benign, is Solitude."
  — *William Wordsworth*

Walking and regular exercise

Just as your heart aches, so does your body.
It is draining to care for your loved one and yourself.

You must maintain your health
in order to effectively meet the demands of your life.

Regular exercise is vital to your well-being.
It releases pent-up feelings and keeps your body strong.

Choose an aerobic activity that you like,
such as walking, bicycling, swimming, jogging, or aerobics
    class.
Make a commitment to fit that activity into your busy
    schedule.
You may want to find an exercise partner or join a class
for mutual support and encouragement.

Check with your physician before you begin,
then build your endurance gradually but surely.

Try to have fun.

Walking may be the simplest and most satisfying choice.
Walk alone or with a friend.
It is excellent exercise and wonderful therapy.

As you walk, the rhythm of your step begins to release
    tension.

Walking focuses your awareness
on yourself as a physical being,
an autonomous person moving through the world
with strength and resiliency.

Your mind begins to clear.
The sinking feeling in the pit of your stomach
 may gradually abate.

Look around you.
Take note of all you see, hear, smell, and feel.

As you begin to exercise more regularly,
you may find that you feel, eat, and sleep better.

As you revitalize yourself through physical activity,
you may discover new sources
of energy and strength within yourself.

Talking . . .

In times of adversity, silence is not golden.
It can make you a prisoner of your own despair.

Seek someone you trust and respect
with whom you can openly share your feelings.

When you put into words
feelings of anxiety, anger, and guilt
you bring them to the surface,
releasing pent-up emotions,
draining unbearable hurt from your heart and soul.

When you let others know
what's really inside of you,
you become less confusing to yourself.

Comfort comes with understanding.

Fear of the future is real.
Do not carry it in silence—or keep it as a secret even from
   yourself.

"Give sorrow words. The grief that does not speak
Whispers the o'er fraught heart and bids it break."
   — *William Shakespeare*

... and listening

Ask, listen, and learn.
Listen to health professionals.
Listen to the experiences and insights of other Alzheimer's
  caregivers.
Listen to the thoughts and feelings of those who love you.
Open your mind to others' views and ideas.

When you ask and listen,
you add new information to your bank of knowledge.

You can hear how others
have approached problems similar to your own.

You can learn how others perceive your words and actions.

You can mull over new ideas,
try them on for size,
alter them to fit your own situation.

We all have two ears and just one mouth.
Perhaps that is so we can listen
twice as much
as we speak.

Avoid wishful hearing.
Neither use your ears to hear what the heart
wants to hear,
nor the mind to filter what your heart
does not wish to admit.

Denying tragedy and conflict is not constructive.

Mental health requires the courage to face harsh realities.
Mental health is the recognition of pain
and the attempt to live with it.

Crying...

When your loved one has Alzheimer's disease
you may feel as if your life
has been ravaged by a sudden raging storm.
Your reality is flooded with sensations of hopelessness
and helplessness.

You may cry out in disbelief:
  "It can't be happening."
You may cry out in horror:
  "Oh my God, there is no cure."
You may cry out in anger:
  "It's not fair."
You may cry out in remorse:
  "If only I had . . ."

The tight hard knot of suffering
may be eased by the shedding of tears.

Crying is an honest expression of a grief that transcends
words.

Crying can release anxiety, dissolve tension, and
help you confront your feelings more clearly.

Everyone experiences and expresses grief in his or her own
way.
Not everyone cries.
That does not mean that the pain is less deeply felt.

Unfortunately, our society places restrictions on
who may choose to cry.
Too often, crying is permissible for women and children,
but not for men.

"Don't be a sissy. Big boys don't cry."
"Take it like a man."

Familiar messages like these have made
many men consider tears a sign of weakness,
of failure, of vulnerability, of lost control.

Crying is a natural expression of aching hearts,
a healthy way to ease anguish and emotional strain.

Repressing our emotions can lead to
psychological harm and physical illness.

If crying is so therapeutic, then
why do men do so little of it?

Good question!

"There is a sacredness in tears.
They are not the mark of weakness, but of power.
They speak more eloquently than ten thousand tongues.
They are messengers of overwhelming grief,
of deep contrition and unspeakable love."

        —Washington Irving

...and laughing

"I smiled today. I even laughed out loud.
I shouldn't be happy. Should I?"

It's okay.
Like crying, laughter helps to release anger and despair.

When you are overwhelmed with anxiety,
your body, mind, and spirit
need a break from impending losses.

Laughter calms and relaxes the body.
It extricates the mind from the frustrations of the day,
permitting the weary spirit to dance freely,
and see the rainbow through the clouds.

The *Journal of the American Medical Association*
reports that laughter has therapeutic value.

Laughter enhances respiration and circulation,
oxygenates blood,
represses stress-related hormones,
and may bolster the immune system.

Learn from children:
a youngster laughs up to five hundred times a day,
an average adult, only fifteen times.

As often as you can,
try to smile, laugh, and enjoy yourself.

Go see a comedy at the movies, or read a funny book.
Reminisce with friends,
recall wonderful humorous events when all was well.

Even in your interactions with your loved one,
there may still be some things
that can make you chuckle.

Reclaim your sense of yourself,
affirm life through laughter and fun.

Gathering memories

How torturous it is
when the person you love
is no longer the person you once knew.

Memories are delicate and fragile.
Try not to lose them in your despair.

Spend time recalling special moments of the past,
particularly times you and your loved one shared together.

You might compile an album or scrapbook
filled with pictures and mementos.
Encourage family and friends to write down
their special remembrances.

Perhaps include a "Laugh Section,"
recalling less serious times together.
When you are reminded of something silly or funny,
add it to your collection.
It will lighten and brighten the days ahead.

Memories are treasures you carry in your heart.
What you once enjoyed, you can never lose.
All that you loved becomes a part of you.

Gathering memories is a way
to celebrate the legacy of the person you knew
and the life you shared.
Even in despair you are saying,
"Thanks for the memory."

Reflections of an Alzheimer's Caregiver

by Cy Moffit

I remember the days when we knew

one another . . .

When we were happy and gay—

Before the Thief of Love's Recognition

Had stolen her heart away.

She has died, but still she lives on,

As she slowly struggles in vain.

How I wish that I could change places

with her,

And end her confusion and pain.

Journal writing

A journal is a place where
you can say anything you wish
without being pitied, judged, criticized,
or made uncomfortable.

There is a difference between writing your thoughts
and speaking them out loud in public.

"Journaling" helps you to express your feelings,
especially when you feel isolated
and find it difficult to communicate with others.

Journals have been called "the paper psychiatrists."

As you write, you unlock layers of feelings,
you explore secret discomforts and new ideas,
you give your thoughts a voice, a concrete presence.
Journal writing can be a deep form of communication with
     yourself.

Pour out your thoughts and feelings.
If you wish, speak them into a cassette recorder.
Write them in a notebook with pen or colored pencils.
Make drawings.
Write poems.

If you use a computer, let your thoughts flow
from your head, down your arms,
through the keyboard to the screen.

Inside you is a story to be told—
no matter how difficult or painful.

You might start by just completing sentences like:
"When I first heard you had Alzheimer's disease . . ."
"There are times when . . ."
"They don't understand that I . . ."
"If only . . ."
"I need . . ."
"I would feel better if . . ."

Don't worry about your writing ability
or knowledge of grammar.
So what if the words seem unprintable or even profane to
     others.
You don't have to share your journal with anyone.
It's yours alone.

Just do what helps you

so that in your inner soul
you can confront and acknowledge
the consequences of Alzheimer's disease in your life

and begin to heal mind and body.

Especially in the anxious dark of night.

Here are some ways you can care for yourself,
as you care for your loved one afflicted with Alzheimer's.

- ✤ Find ways to have others take turns caring for the
  Alzheimer's patient.
  Share the responsibility with paid caregivers
  or other friends or family members.

- ✤ Seek information and ideas about the issues of
  caretaking.
  Talk to people who have had firsthand experience.
  Listen with an open mind,
  then try out those ideas that make sense to you.

- ✤ Get out of the house when you can.
  Fresh air, change of scenery, and exercise
  can help you make connections with a world beyond.

- ✤ If you can't get out of the house, use the phone
  to keep in contact with friends.

- ✤ Stay in touch with your own feelings.
  Cry if you wish.
  Keep a journal, draw, write poetry, meditate.

- Eat well. Get enough sleep. Exercise.

- Don't give up pastimes that used to give you pleasure.

- Take time to relive memories of special times
  you and your loved one shared.

- Balance your own needs with those of your loved one.
  Try to find a "happy medium."

- Give yourself treats; plan plenty of perks for yourself.

- Maintain your sense of humor. Try to laugh every day.

- Plan minivacations every day, lasting for even half
  an hour.
  Go for a walk, listen to music, take a long bath.

- Plan a real vacation several times a year, if you can.

- If you feel you are approaching a breaking point,
  get professional help.

chapter

3

FINDING SUPPORT:
FAMILY, FRIENDS, AND OTHERS

Almost eighty percent of Alzheimer's disease caregivers
report high levels of stress-induced
physical and psychological ailments.

These can be desperately trying times.
You must give yourself permission
to solicit and accept the help of others
during the roller-coaster course
of your loved one's illness.

Remember:
Receiving is the other side of giving—
and equally important
in creating and maintaining bonds
of love and caring.

Receiving support from your family

The tragedy of Alzheimer's disease
can bring the members of your family closer together.

Alzheimer's disease can also drive your family apart.

Just as reactions in the family have differed
at other times and in other situations,
so will responses to this disease.

Each person's relationship with the afflicted family member
is unique and different.

You cannot write a script for the other members of your
    family to follow.
They cannot write one for you.

One caregiver recalls,

"For a long time, my father was more erratic in my presence
than he was when he was with my brother.
For that reason, we disagreed on the type of care our father
needed.
My brother felt that the current arrangements were still
acceptable,
while I thought the time had come to place my father in a
nursing home."

Even when all members of the family observe the same
behavior,
people will have different opinions about the best response.

Difficult as it may be,
try to see life
from the perspective of your siblings and other relatives.

Do more than understand.
Change places with them in your mind and imagination.

Enter their lives;
stand in their shoes.

When you are angry and troubled,
remember that you can never know what other family
    members are feeling
any more than they can know what you are experiencing.

Remember that there are no perfect relationships,
especially with chronic illness in the family.

You are human; so are they.
You disappoint; so do they.
When you do and they do, the hurt, the anger,
the feelings of betrayal,
are magnified many times.

Try to accept the members of your family
for what they are and are not.
You may all need to adjust your expectations
as you accept
each other's strengths and shortcomings.

Very often, one family member assumes responsibility as
    primary caregiver.
When this decision is dictated by circumstances rather than
    choice,
resentments can run high.

The families that cope most effectively
with Alzheimer's disease
are those who share their feelings and discuss their
    problems
clearly and openly,
without hostility.

It is very important that caregiving responsibilities and roles
are discussed, agreed upon, and honestly acknowledged
by all family members.

As you identify and divide tasks,
and consider options
for meeting your loved one's needs,
listen to one another carefully.

Respect honest differences of opinion.

Accept compromises.

Be aware that unfinished family business
can complicate
the issues you are confronting today.

Unresolved quarrels and resentments from your childhood
may still lurk like monsters in the closet,
casting their shadows
on current family discussions and controversies.

Do your best to heal past wounds.

Your pain as a child need not be
your pain as an adult.

Mourn your past if you must,
but now try to extricate yourself from its grip.

Make time to be together with your family.

Share the joys and triumphs of your lives
as well as your burdens.

Create happy memories and strengthen your love
by planning good times together,
as well as gathering to discuss the somber responsibility
of caring for your loved one.

You all need support, understanding, and love
as together you face
the uncertain and painful future.

"For hatred does not cease by hatred
at any time; hatred ceases by love.
That is the Eternal law."
—The Dhammapada

What about the children?

You may be part of
the "sandwiched generation,"
with responsibilities both to aging relatives
and to growing children.

Perhaps you have opened your home to an ailing parent.

Perhaps you wonder how often
you should take your children with you
to visit your loved one who is suffering from Alzheimer's
  disease.

Just as you cannot protect adults from sickness and pain,
you cannot shield children from traumatic experiences.

Good mental health is not the denial of illness and tragedy,
but the frank acknowledgment of the situation and the
    sorrow.

Helping children to understand and cope
with Alzheimer's disease in the family
is a difficult but extremely important task.

It is an ongoing commitment
to talk and listen to one another.

In words that your children can understand,
explain what Alzheimer's disease is
and how it may affect your family.

Tell them the truth.

If a relative who shares a home with you is stricken with
    Alzheimer's,
there will be serious issues for your whole family to face.

If you choose to bring a loved one with Alzheimer's into
    your home
in order to offer adequate care,
this decision will affect the lives of *all* family members.

Encourage your children to talk
about whatever is on their minds,
even if the thoughts are painful to you.

Listen not only to your children's words
but also to the messages conveyed in their behavior.

Perhaps:

They feel left out, frightened, neglected, and angry
because you devote so much of yourself and your time
to the person who is sick.

They are angry at the person with Alzheimer's disease
for ruining everyone else's life.

They are confused, upset, and humiliated
by the person with Alzheimer's disease
who may call them by their parent's name,
repeat the same demand over and over,
or accuse them of stealing valuable possessions.

They are embarrassed to have their friends over
because of their relative's unpredictable behavior.

Try to address the problems with compassion.
Acknowledge that this is a difficult time for the whole
     family.

Let your children know that they can share
their true feelings, fears, and fantasies
and that together,
as a family,
you will try to find ways to make life less stressful.

Make special efforts to stay close to your children.
Plan family outings. Play and laugh together.
Be available when they want to talk.
Hug them.
Provide extra attention, praise, and emotional support.

Your children can be a tremendous source
of vitality, joy, solace, and love.

Be open to the emotional strength they can offer you.

Demonstrate clearly
that despite this terrible disease,
they are valued and loved.

If you are visiting a relative or friend with Alzheimer's
     disease,
prepare your children in advance
for the changes they will see and notice.

Silence and secrecy
heighten their sense of being shut out
and may cause them
to imagine dreadful things that are not so.

For example, children may feel that in some way
they are responsible
for the illness
or the family despair.

They may fear that you,
their parent,
will also get the disease.

A daughter of an Alzheimer's patient shares her experience.

"Your kids need to know what to expect.
They need to know that it's ALWAYS okay to ask.
If anything interests or bothers them,
if there's something they don't understand,
asking is a good thing to do."

Remember that it is natural
for children to become restless
with long visits to the hospital or nursing home.

Remember that it is natural
for them to feel uncomfortable
with a dementing disease.

Share some of your feelings with your children.
Your ability to express your anguish and confusion
will help your children find
the words and voice
to express their own emotions.

Your children will begin to understand
that the fear, resentment, and sorrow
they may be experiencing
is a normal manifestation of grief.

There are groups and resources that can help you address
the concern you feel about your children
and the fear and anger your children may have toward the
    Alzheimer's patient
and the changes this terrible disease has brought into their
    lives.

Some books and organizations are listed in the Resources
    section at the back of this book.

Alzheimer's disease is a crisis
shared by ALL members of the family.

By facing the sad reality and mourning it together,
you may help your children—
and yourself—
grow as caring, capable, and creative individuals
who understand and treasure
the honesty, trust, love, and support
that can be nurtured within a family.

Receiving support from friends

Bearing the burden of Alzheimer's disease
intensifies feelings of isolation.
The dull devastating ache of loneliness
can become overwhelming.

The importance of friends
during this time of misfortune and upheaval
cannot be overstated.

When withdrawal seems like the easy road to travel,
let friends keep you in touch with life.

Their continuing care and love will bring you comfort and
consolation.

You may think your friends are avoiding you,
as if they feel the tragedy of Alzheimer's disease is
    contagious.

Unfortunately, this sometimes happens.

Many of us do not know how to respond
when tragedy and grief
strike those we care for.

Your friends may feel paralyzed
by not knowing what to say or what to do.

Rather than offend you
by doing something inappropriate or insensitive,
they may disappear or do nothing at all.

Some friends may (often mistakenly)
believe it is an intrusion
to call you
when you're beset by so many uncertainties.

Some friends may be terrified by the specter of
physical and mental illness.
They don't want to feel vulnerable.
They don't want to think about the fragility of life.

They may be particularly anxious about Alzheimer's
   disease,
knowing that it could also strike their own families—
even themselves.

Try to be patient and understanding with your friends.

You may need to take the initiative
and help them overcome their discomfort,
to feel at ease with you again.

Invite them into your home.
Be honest.
Share your emotions and needs.
Do not give in to misplaced feelings of shame.

You don't need to hide your thoughts from real friends.

Friends are not mind readers.
They cannot be expected
to always say the right thing
or to instinctively understand your pain.

Sometimes a person's soothing words,
however well intended,
may wound and offend you.

Someone may say:
> Count your blessings. You had so many wonderful years
> together.

You may want to shout:
> I don't feel blessed, I feel robbed!
> We should have had so many, many more wonderful
> years together.
> Maybe someday I'll relish what we shared in the past.
> But not now.
> I'm terrified of what's happening in the present!

Someone may say:

It'll be okay. You'll be fine. You just need to go on with your life.

You may want to shout:

It's not going to be okay or fine.

Don't you know that Alzheimer's disease didn't just invade my loved one's life? It invaded my life as well!

Alzheimer's is a progressive disease with no cure.

It grows worse and worse, for BOTH of us.

Someone may say:

I could never handle this as well as you.

You may want to shout:

Don't put me on a pedestal. I'm not perfect.

I make lots of mistakes.

There's no good way to handle this grotesque disease.

What I want to do is scream and wail at the injustice.

I want my life back!

I want my loved one back!

Words never suffice when pain runs as deep as the ocean.
There's no quick fix.

There's a difference between
being saved and
being supported.

What you need from friends is
the permission and opportunity
to be yourself.

Choose and seek out friends who will

- listen to how you feel, and not tell you how you should feel

- continue to call and visit, even when you are in a rotten mood

- not overwhelm you with their presence but allow spaces in your togetherness

- help you have fun and relax, even in the face of Alzheimer's disease

- offer nonjudgmental, compassionate support

You can help your friends
by being specific about your needs:

"Could you pick my kids up after school?
I need to be at the nursing home."

Listen to their advice. It may be helpful.
But remember to always do what's right for you.

Tell them when they've helped
and how much you appreciate them.
Having someone who cares means a great deal.

When help is not forthcoming or sufficient,
seek additional assistance from other sources:
    other friends and family members
    professional services
    support groups

People need people.
Friends need friends.
We all need *support*.

Alzheimer's disease support groups

For many caregivers, Alzheimer's support groups
are a lifeline.

Alzheimer's support groups often include
regular meetings, buddy systems,
crisis phone lines, and special groups for children.
The phone numbers and addresses listed in the Resources
section
at the back of this book will help you locate a group near
your home.

In a support group, you are no longer isolated.

You are traveling a path in the company of others
whose circumstances are similar to your own.

Each person has reached
different points along the route,
and will share the road map of his or her journey.

As you compare notes,
you will find relief in knowing that your
intense feelings are not unique.

Where else can you share
scary and troubling feelings
of anger, resentment, coldness, and shame,
and hear from others that these are
natural and normal reactions to Alzheimer's disease?

Where else can you exchange
practical, creative ideas
for dealing with daily issues of Alzheimer's caregiving:
the patient's personal hygiene,
inappropriate behavior, and safety?

Alzheimer's support group members understand
when you ask,
   "Why me?"

They understand when you say,
   "I don't think I can make it."

In an Alzheimer's disease support group,
you can weep without feeling embarrassed,
laugh without feeling guilt.

You can voice your fears, your loss, and your despair.
And others can truly say,
   "I know how you feel."

Alzheimer's support groups
provide the compassionate network
of a "second family."

In a nonjudgmental atmosphere of trust and caring,
you can explore sensitive issues
with other caregivers
who have similar experiences and concerns.

You can talk about your changing feelings
toward your loved one
who may now seem like a stranger.

Do you still love this person who has become a patient?
Or is the one you love already gone?
When memories and the ability to communicate are gone,
when those unique character traits
that made your loved one so special have disappeared,
what remains?

You can discuss difficult issues
of sexuality and couplehood.

Does your spouse still want to make love with you?
Do you still want to be a lover to your ailing spouse?
Perhaps you'd like to pursue a new love relationship,
but you have conflicted feelings.
Would you be betraying your loyalty
to your afflicted wife or husband?

There are no correct answers to these intimate questions.

But voicing your thoughts and fears to others
who care about you
and who understand the complexity of your situation
can help you find your way to your own solution,
the answer that feels right or best to you.

Sharing is healing,
and you help when you share.

"For we desire nothing
but to share
the grief, and make it
easier to bear."

— *Geoffrey Chaucer*

Professional counseling

When a loved one has Alzheimer's disease
it is normal and understandable
that you have feelings of
anger, despair, and helplessness.

There may be times when you need someone
other than a friend, family, or support group
to help you confront and cope with the
devastating effects of this mind-destroying illness.

It may be too painful
or too embarrassing
to talk about certain feelings or pose certain questions
to those who are close to you.

Your physician can refer you to
a professional counselor who will help you
come to terms with your feelings,
examine alternatives, and make choices.

He or she can help you gain and maintain
your balance through this troubling time.

It is possible, though very difficult, to be
an involved caregiver without burning out.

It requires a network of support, and
a great deal of patience, understanding, flexibility,
compassion, and commitment
on everyone's part.

Professional counseling is not a substitute
for friends or family sustenance,
but another helpful support system
for you to rely on.

Some professional counselors are specially trained
to work with all the victims of Alzheimer's disease,
patients, caregivers, and families.

They can help you cope with your own emotions
and manage your conflicting obligations,
as well as locate resources
and suggest strategic interventions for your loved one.

Consult the Alzheimer's Disease and Education Referral
    Center
or your local family and community health agencies for
an appropriate referral.

Professional counseling and support is a recommended
    option if you

- ↤ feel the agony is just too hard to bear

- ↤ find yourself playing the role of martyr,
    feeling that only you can provide the right kind of
    caregiving

- ↤ find that you are taking out your feelings of rage and
    frustration on the Alzheimer's patient

- ↤ feel abandoned by doctors, family, and friends

- ↤ feel increased hostility toward people you once cared
    for a great deal

- ↤ feel humiliated by your loved one's bizarre behavior
    and don't know how to handle this feeling

- ↤ find that you are avoiding all outside contact and
    activities, preferring to be by yourself or alone with
    the Alzheimer's patient

↬   know that your physical health is suffering
    from the stress and demands of caregiving

↬   are relying more and more on alcohol, drugs, or both

↬   feel trapped in emotions of hostility, recrimination,
    and melancholy
    that increase, rather than diminish, over time

↬   have constant feelings of depression: hopelessness or
    helplessness;
    an inability to eat, sleep, or work;
    overwhelming feelings of failure, guilt, rage, and
    insecurity;
    thoughts of suicide

In general:
    If you feel stuck in a caregiving situation that is
        not working
        and feel unable to find alternatives,

    if you are alarmed or unhappy or dissatisfied
        with the ways you are behaving and reacting,

    it is wise and responsible to seek professional advice and
        assistance.

Spiritual support

If you believe in a Higher Power,
like the one some of us call God,
Alzheimer's disease may leave you feeling
betrayed or alienated.

Spiritual beliefs are often challenged
during life crises.

God may appear distant and removed,
too far away to be of help.

Some people believe that if you live a truly spiritual
    existence,
"goodness and mercy
will follow you all the days of your life."

It's NOT TRUE.

Religion is not an insurance policy
offering protection
against the cruel blows of sickness.

Religion does not preclude grief
nor inoculate you against suffering.

Doubts are part of the cycle of faith.

"Dear God, why me? Why us?"

It is natural in our scientific world
to seek answers and explanations.

Know this:
No one understands why
good people go through such torturous times.

God doesn't hand out prizes
based on how well you've behaved.

"Dear God, why me? Why us?"

You may rage at God because
of the cruelty inflicted on
you and your loved ones
by this lingering, crippling disease.

Honest anger could be your form of prayer.

You cannot be angry at nothing.
No one can hurt you like those closest to you and those you
    most trust.

To be furious at God could indicate
that there is a "God-Force" in your life
that is real and meaningful.

Your wrath may be evidence
that God was once present in your life

and may be again.

"Dear God, why me? Why us?"

You may think that God is punishing you.

You may look inward to find
the justification for these new, painful events in your life
in a kind of Divine Chastisement
    for not attending religious services regularly
    for doing things of which you are not proud.

Alzheimer's disease has nothing to do
with rewards and punishments.

You and your loved one are not being disciplined
and are not responsible for the illness.

"Dear God, why me? Why us?"

Blaming God is a natural and normal response
to extreme anguish.

Many spiritual leaders have felt this way.
Jesus said,
> "My God, my God,
> Why hast thou forsaken me?"

It's okay to be angry at God.
God can take it.

In the book *The Dying Child*, Dr. John Easson tells of a
> young patient saying,
> "If God is God, He will understand my anger.
> If He cannot understand my anger,
> He cannot be God."

What a powerful confession of faith!

"Dear God, why me? Why us?"

When a woman learned that her husband had Alzheimer's
    disease
she said that her spiritual pain was so great
that she felt like Jacob
wrestling with the angel.

In the midst of her suffering
she found a comforting presence in a power
greater than herself.
No longer did she have to struggle alone
"in the valley of the shadows."

With faith and doubts, she quoted Elie Wiesel,
    "God is the answers . . .
    and the questions too."

"Dear God, why me? Why us?"

It may be not only a question but
also your cry of distress,
your plea for help.

When unexpected crises shatter life,
and anxiety and grief become the fabric of your days,
your faith may flicker low
and become extinguished.

However, for some,
facing illness can also be a religious pilgrimage.

Faith can somehow be strengthened through the painful
        struggle,
and both comfort in spiritual beliefs
and a holiness—in Hebrew, *Kedusha*—
with deeper insights and new understandings
can be found.

Faith may help you
accept the unacceptable,

giving you courage and compassion
as you support your loved one
through the limbo
of this disease.

Through prayers, simple or formal,
you can release your feelings,
and utter your secret concerns and fears.

In the darkness of your anguish,
you may discover a measure of solace and peace,
a sense that even as you struggle,
you do not struggle alone.

Prayer of Faith

(author unknown)

We trust that beyond absence,

there is a presence.

That beyond the pain,

there can be healing.

That beyond the brokenness,

there can be wholeness.

That beyond the anger,

there may be peace.

That beyond the hurting,

there may be forgiveness.

That beyond the silence,

there may be the word.

That beyond the word,

there may be understanding.

That through understanding,

there is love.

ↄ
chapter
4

Achieving Compassion and Forgiveness

Alzheimer's disease has created a different world
for you and your loved one;
a world of conflicted feelings—
hope and despair,
acceptance and terror—
with tears both shed and unshed.

Can anything good
come from the heartbreak of this ordeal?

"Those things that hurt, instruct."
— *Benjamin Franklin*

Being an Alzheimer's disease caregiver
forces you to ask yourself hard questions
about the meaning and purpose of your own life.

"Who am I really?"
"What do I now want out of life?"
"How do I get through this torment?"
"Where can I go for support during these troubled times?"
"What is the meaning of my existence?"

Through the trials of caregiving,
through the torment of witnessing the devastation of this
    disease,
you gain new perspective.

You begin to rethink priorities,
refine your goals,
and redefine your future.

New perspectives

Caring for parents and other family members with
    Alzheimer's disease,
especially when you are in your middle years,
can be a harbinger of your own future,
a foreshadowing of your own elderly self.

You may be confronted with fears of your own mortality—
loss of youth, loss of physical and mental abilities,
loss of economic and social status,
a fear fed by society's
denial of the natural aging process.

Moving beyond denial gives you
both the challenge and the opportunity
to grow into older age,
rather than merely falling into it,

to explore and address
the possibilities of how best
to live these years of your life.

For caregivers of all ages,
the uncertainty of Alzheimer's disease
almost compels a new mental flexibility.

Old goals, dreams, and hopes,
former values and standards,
must adjust to new realities dictated by the disease.

What was supremely significant at one time
may become insignificant and almost trivial in the present.

You are able to take a longer view of the illness.
You reassign priorities,
and dismiss that which is no longer possible.

As you continue to care for your loved one,
you must often negotiate and compromise,
accepting your own limitations
and the limitations of others.

Through these experiences, you grow.
You learn to listen, understand, and forgive.

You grow more tolerant, more patient,
more open-minded, more understanding,
more compassionate.

You feel a kinship with others
suffering pain and loss.

What a rich inner life,
spiritual capacity, and wisdom
can be accumulated from these trials.

"Without the valleys there would be no mountains.
And if you don't scale the mountains,
you don't see the view."
      —*Anonymous*

Accepting change

You must now focus on adjusting to a new life script
in which you and your loved one
play different parts.

Family roles shift radically when one member
is stricken with Alzheimer's.
As a caregiver, you must let go of expectations that are no
    longer viable.
You must find ways to redistribute responsibilities,
acquire new skills,
and establish new relationships, personal and practical,
that help you meet the demands of your new life.

As the realities of your relationship with your loved one
    change,
your feelings will too.

A caregiver recalls the shifts in her feelings toward her
    father
during his long illness.

"I *loved* my father.
But though this man appeared to be my father,
his essence was gone.

He really wasn't my father.

As time passed,
I found myself feeling more and more removed—at times
    cold.
I hated the feeling—I wanted things to be as they had been,
to somehow turn back the clock,

but of course I couldn't."

One of the most difficult challenges that faces an
    Alzheimer's disease caregiver
is to create a new relationship
with your loved one despite the mental deterioration.

The sense of detachment described by the caregiver above
is a common, normal, healthy response.

Alzheimer's disease robs a patient of his or her selfhood.
Memories of shared experiences are gone.
Unique attributes of the person you loved have disappeared.
He or she is no longer capable of being an equal partner
in a loving relationship.

Yet individuals do not consist of memories alone.
You also have feelings and perceptions that exist in the
    present.
It is in these realms that you can still, at times, communicate
with the ones you love.

One such treasured moment is recalled by the daughter
of an Alzheimer's patient.

"Dad is eating soup at the table.
Ori is a toddler. He travels around the table,
holding firmly to the edge.

"When he comes to Dad, he opens his mouth,
like a baby bird looking for food.
Dad understands, chuckles,
and spoons soup carefully into Ori's mouth."

Compassion and understanding

A caregiver speaks of the lessons
that she learned from her ordeal with Alzheimer's.

"First you need to get past the *details:*
the mixed-up clothing, the loss of privacy,
the financial arrangements;

past the *loss:*
of a give-and-take relationship
with your loved one;

past the *disappointment*
of a lingering future unlike the one you had planned;

even past the *jealousy*
of seeing other mothers and daughters
in roles for which you yearn.

Mom and the staff at the Alzheimer's Center
helped us fully understand what was left
once you got past all that heartbreak

—the joy of unconditional love.

The world of an Alzheimer's patient teaches us a basic tenet
—everyone needs to feel loved and special.

It all sounds so simplistic,
but it was so evident in the Alzheimer's patient's world
and too often absent in ours."

Forgiving and healing

You are making peace with
the past and present,
that unfinished anger, pain, and
resentment.

What has happened or is occurring
cannot be changed.

You cannot alter the disease.

Love is too precious to be lost.
Pride should not stand in the way of reconciliation.

You are learning to forgive.

To forgive means

to give yourself the opportunity to place behind you
the agonies that diminish your strength,
diminish your being;

to give yourself
new energies to move on to meet new challenges;

to give yourself
the courage and resignation to live
in an unfair,
disappointing world.

Forgiveness is the victory of love, compassion,
and mercy over anger.

Living remembrances

Incorporate the values and passions
that you cherished in your loved one
into your own life.
Make them part of your being, your philosophy, your faith.
Pass them on to others.

Create in this way a living memorial to your loved one,
keeping his or her essence and spirit alive,
bringing comfort and meaning to yourself and others.

"And yes I said yes I will yes."
— *James Joyce*

Turning toward tomorrow

You now realize that health
and life are not forever.

You are looking at your own life differently,
suddenly realizing that you
are but a visitor upon Earth.
Like Emily in the last act of *Our Town,*
you now know that life is both
temporary and precious.

The humdrum world should never be
taken for granted.

As perceptions grow, you are imbued
with a sudden sense of energy.

Each day is a new beginning.

Good feelings are your birthright, too.

How you wish you might have changed
your own lifestyle and
your relationship to your loved one.

So many regrets, recriminations.
So much you might have done differently.

But you're human.
No one always does the right things
at the right time.
No one!

So, you're not perfect.
But under the circumstances, you're
doing the best you can, aren't you?

If your loved one were able,
perhaps he or she would thank you.
Be proud of yourself.
Pat yourself on the back.

Rabbi Zusya said that on the day of judgment,
God would not ask him why
he had not been like Moses,
but rather why he had not been Zusya.

The journey ahead is unknown,
but you are learning to survive,
continuing on the best you can
with the tools and strength at your disposal.

Even with the tragic certainties
and uncertainties of Alzheimer's disease,
life is still an adventure.

"Keep a green tree in your heart,
and perhaps the singing bird will come."
— *Chinese proverb*

Finding strength within yourself

Alzheimer's disease, I do not like you.
Not at all.

But now that you have
intruded into the life of my family,
I will learn to live with you.

You ARE powerful.
Your cruel winds have bruised
and buffeted me.
Yet, you will never defeat me.

I will face you, lean into you,
storm back at you,
and find my own strength.

I will accept this terrible mind-altering illness,
reshape my life,
change, and grow.

But Alzheimer's disease, you cannot cripple my love,
suppress memories of what we shared,
silence courage,
or conquer my spirit.

"I can never lose one whom I have loved unto the end;
one to whom my soul cleaves so firmly
that it can never be separated,
does not go away but only goes before."
— *St. Bernard of Clairvaux*

~~~
chapter
5
~~~

QUESTIONS AND ANSWERS ABOUT ALZHEIMER'S

CHAPTER 5 DRAWS ON MY EXPERIENCE (KENNETH S. KOSIK, M.D.) AS
A PRACTICING PHYSICIAN AND RESEARCHER. THE PRACTICAL QUES-
TIONS THAT ARISE FOR THE CAREGIVER FACING ALZHEIMER'S DISEASE
GO FAR BEYOND THE MATERIAL PRESENTED HERE, BUT THIS CHAPTER
PROVIDES A STARTING POINT. THE ORGANIZATIONS AND PUBLICA-
TIONS LISTED IN THE RESOURCES SECTION OFFER MORE DETAILED
INFORMATION.

WHEN AN AGING PERSON FORGETS, IS IT ALZHEIMER'S?

Because Alzheimer's disease is so common among the elderly,
many people live in fear of getting this illness. Every time they forget
a name, miss an appointment, or neglect to pick up a particular item
from the market, they fear that the disease is beginning to affect them.
But in fact the tendency to falter a bit over recalling names and other
details is nearly universal among elders and is not related to Alzheimer's disease. Physicians call mild memory loss in people over fifty
age-associated memory loss. People who feel some decline in their
memory function and are formally tested may show a very small

impairment. This condition can be gracefully accepted as a normal part of life.

WHAT IS THE DIFFERENCE BETWEEN NORMAL FORGETFULNESS AND ALZHEIMER'S DISEASE?

Everyone forgets. We could not function if our minds did not screen out the forgettable, like the temperature on this day last year or the color of socks we wore one week ago.

Sometimes, though, under the most ordinary circumstances, we forget things we should remember. For example, you are dashing out the door and your spouse says, "Don't forget to stop for a loaf of bread on the way home." Moments after you return empty-handed, the memory of that reminder comes rushing back. This is called a failure of registration: you simply weren't paying enough attention for the request to stick. Paying attention is a prerequisite to the formation of any memory. In this case, the failure to pay attention made the memory fragile, so that you could retrieve it only when it was cued by the original context, the return home. Alzheimer's disease does not cause this kind of memory loss.

Your ability to recall, say, a list of words after a few minutes is called short-term memory. Short-term memory is basically equivalent to learning. This form of memory is the most affected by Alzheimer's disease. The inability to recall over the short term is why Alzheimer's patients often repeat themselves.

The ability to recollect past experiences and feelings is called long-term memory. The effect of Alzheimer's disease on long-term memory is complex. Even when the mind is working normally, the memories that we retain over the long term may seem like a disconnected patchwork. Alzheimer's patients retain many of their long-term memories, but sometimes the distant past inappropriately intrudes into the present. For example, when asked about his occupation, one of my patients mentioned a job he had held several decades ago for a brief time, overlooking the work he had done for most of his life. Or, when asked the name of her spouse, another patient named her high school sweetheart. Likewise, when I asked a woman who had been married for more than forty years her name, she told me her maiden name.

Mild short-term memory loss alone may not be due to Alzheimer's, but may represent only age-associated memory loss. Alzheimer's disease differs in that it is progressive and affects other brain functions besides memory, such as thinking processes, personality, and perception. Sometimes these changes occur even before memory loss begins.

A Case: Alzheimer's disease affects more than memory

At his wife's insistence, Mr. B came in to see me. She was worried about the trouble he encountered in putting a key into a lock, and then opening the door. He also had difficulty in planning a simple sequence such as how to get his car out of their single-lane driveway when her car was blocking his. As I asked more questions, it became apparent that his memory for appointments had begun to falter and that he often repeated himself. A well-dressed man in his early sixties who carried himself with dignity, he quite articulately insisted that nothing was wrong with him. But over the ensuing years Mr. B developed all the symptoms of Alzheimer's disease. At the disease's onset his memory was only minimally affected, but instead he lost his spatial ability—his ability to orient and manipulate a key in a lock, for example, or to move one car first to make way for a second.

How do we know that it's Alzheimer's disease?

Often, by simply talking to the patient, performing a physical examination, checking the patient's cognitive abilities, and doing a few laboratory tests, the doctor can make a diagnosis of Alzheimer's disease with a confidence level of approximately ninety percent, meaning that the diagnosis will be correct in nine out of ten cases. Because the condition of Alzheimer's patients deteriorates over time, the physician can increase the certainty of the diagnosis by seeing the person at six-month intervals.

Testing for Alzheimer's disease involves a few blood tests, often a brain scan, and sometimes a neuropsychological evaluation, which tests a person's memory, problem-solving ability, and use of language. None of these tests can prove a person has Alzheimer's disease, although recently some tests have become available, which suggest the diagnosis. However, these tests are not much better than a thorough medical evaluation. One of the most important reasons to evaluate a person with dementia is to discover whether a diagnosis other than Alzheimer's disease might explain the symptoms and, if so, whether dementia can be treated. Unfortunately, treatable causes of dementia are rare. The doctor may discover that the dementia is caused by the patient's medications; side effects from a surprisingly large number of drugs can result in symptoms of dementia.

The medical evaluation for Alzheimer's disease is not terribly time-consuming, not at all painful, and easy for the doctor to perform. If you or someone you know is worried about having the disease, it is worth getting the few tests required. Your fears may well be laid to rest. There is nothing to be ashamed of in mentioning your worries to a physician or a nurse.

A Case: Sometimes patients can mask the disease

Mr. J came to see me at his wife's insistence. She was very concerned about certain changes in her husband's memory and behavior, but she did not want to say much in front of him because she feared he would become annoyed. He was a charming, physically fit man of sixty-eight who had retired one year before, but who remained active playing golf and bridge. He had a wide circle of friends and continued to entertain them with his good sense of humor. During my exam I asked him some routine questions in order to determine the soundness of his thinking processes. He correctly told me the name of his college, his various employers, the current month and season. But when I asked him what year it was, he said 1959! He was wrong by more than thirty years.

People with early Alzheimer's disease can continue to perform familiar tasks and behaviors. For example, Mr. J had a repertoire of jokes that he told many times and he remained popular at cocktail parties. Adept at masking his disease socially and skilled at taking cues from others, he laughed at the right times even when he did not always follow party banter. His job as a company executive, however, was very demanding, and his choice to retire was probably an early response to the symptoms of the disease.

How does the disease progress?

The long journey between the diagnosis and the more advanced stages of the disease usually lasts about ten years, but it can vary greatly. A decade is the average time from diagnosis to death. In the end, patients usually become bedridden and highly susceptible to pneumonia, which is the most common cause of death in Alzheimer's patients. By the time pneumonia sets in, patients are often completely unable to care for themselves.

Before that final stage, Alzheimer's disease extends its destruction beyond a failed memory. Patients may lose their ability to find their way around, first in unfamiliar settings and later in their own homes. They lose nearly all sense of time: they may prepare breakfast at dinner time, or assume it is time for breakfast regardless of what time they awake. They may wander outside in the middle of the night. They lose the ability to recognize objects and so may no longer be able to use a key or a fork. A wastebasket or a fireplace may be mistaken for a toilet. Their ability to use language, particularly names, begins to fail, and the words they speak may seem empty and devoid of meaning. They lose interest in hobbies and events going on around them. They may stop participating in conversations and even become disinclined to speak at all.

Their personality may also change. Alzheimer's patients often get angry, although their outbursts are brief. They frequently become paranoid and accuse others of stealing their possessions. This suspicion leads to a vicious circle in which an Alzheimer's patient hides money or valuables, forgets where the objects are hidden, and then becomes convinced that the belongings have been stolen.

As the disease progresses, and Alzheimer's patients require help with feeding, bathing, and going to the bathroom, certain physical symptoms develop. Patients may hold their arms, legs, and neck very tightly; they seem unable to relax their muscles. Sometimes they will make quick jerking movements over which they have no control, and possibly no awareness. At this point, when the peaceful sleep of pneumonia ends the ordeal, it is clear why pneumonia has been called "an old person's friend."

A Case: A late stage of the disease

Ms. Z had been in a nursing home for four years and had been diagnosed with Alzheimer's disease five years before that time. Her daughter's decision to place Ms. Z in a nursing home had been difficult, because she knew that no institution could ever know her mother's likes and dislikes the way she did. Now she visited her mother every day and arranged for someone to give her mother a daily massage. Ms. Z's condition was distressing: she no longer even seemed to recognize her daughter. She did not speak, and her limbs were stiff. She was confined to bed except when the staff propped her up in a chair. She had to be fed. But there were brief moments that made her daughter wonder how much Ms. Z still felt. Last week, she told me that her mother opened her eyes wide, and there for an instant was the old sparkle and, remarkably, an unmistakable look of recognition.

WHAT SHOULD I DO IF MY LOVED ONE NO LONGER RECOGNIZES ME?

Alzheimer's disease attacks the ability to recognize once familiar people. We take for granted the special type of perception that allows us to distinguish even subtle differences among faces, to pick out a familiar face in a crowd. This ability develops from a very young age when babies fix their attention on well-known faces.

If your loved one fails to recognize your face, she may still know your voice. Approach her from the front and address her by name, so as not to startle her. Maintain eye contact and speak slowly using concrete words. Because so much communication stems from the emotional tone of your words and body language, try to be aware of the impression you are making on her. It can be profoundly confusing when someone who it is impossible for the patient to recall acts very chummy: accepting such behavior from someone who seems to be a complete stranger must certainly be uncomfortable for the patient.

A Case of lost identity

Every Friday night, Mr. M had dinner with his parents. After his father died, he continued the custom for many years with his mother, Ms. M. In her late seventies she became forgetful, and as her condition worsened it became apparent that she had Alzheimer's disease. One evening after dinner Mr. M returned his mother back to her apartment and, as was his custom, helped her to open the door, and proceeded to leave. But this time she became amorous and seemed offended when he did not come in. She wanted to know why he was leaving her, and she reached out to touch him as she had formerly touched his father. Mr. M realized that his mother was confusing him with her husband. For her, the conclusion of each of these dinners became a painful reenactment of abandonment.

WHAT HAPPENS IN THE BRAIN OF A PERSON WITH ALZHEIMER'S DISEASE?

Years before the onset of any symptoms, as much as one or even two decades before there is the slightest hint of the disease, a small peptide (a combination of amino acids, the building blocks of proteins) called ß-amyloid begins to accumulate within the brain. Normally, we all have exceedingly small amounts of this peptide circulating in our bloodstream and spinal fluid. In the disease, ß-amyloid molecules clump together to form first a loose mesh, and then an increasingly dense mesh of filaments that insert themselves among the many delicate nerve endings in the brain. These deposits are called *senile plaques* and represent one of the principal hallmarks of the disease. After the patient's death, pathologists look for these microscopic structures during the postmortem examination. But senile plaques alone are not sufficient to make possible a diagnosis of Alzheimer's disease.

The other change in a brain affected with Alzheimer's disease, and the other microscopic structure for which pathologists search, is the *neurofibrillary tangle*. Neurofibrillary tangles form when a highly resistant protein becomes concentrated within the nerve cells. Eventually nerve cells choke as the tangle crowds out the cells' contents. The tangle itself sometimes remains behind once the cell around it dies, earning the eerie names "tombstones" or "ghost tangles." Not surprisingly, the parts of the brain most affected by the tangles are those that deal with memory and emotion.

A Case: Sometimes the disease seems dormant until a tragedy tips you over the edge

Three years ago, when Mr. D was in his early eighties and still working part-time, he lost his son in a tragic automobile accident. After his son's death he had trouble concentrating and seemed to lose interest in his work. A few months later, he sometimes seemed disoriented in his own neighborhood, and more than once he could not recall where he had parked his car. Nevertheless, he lived alone and managed to care for himself, although he paid somewhat less attention to his personal hygiene. Because his symptoms were getting worse, Mr. D's brothers brought him into the clinic for an evaluation. The diagnosis was Alzheimer's disease.

The Alzheimer's disease process begins many years before patients or their families actually observe symptoms. As long as the environment and family situation are the same, the disease may remain undetected. But Alzheimer's patients are ill equipped to deal with new settings and situations, and when faced with change, the disease often becomes apparent. (This is why we try to keep Alzheimer's patients out of the hospital; the unfamiliar setting aggravates the condition and can make the patient confused and disoriented.) Mr. D's personal tragedy occurred during this long latent period and led his family to think that his son's death caused his disease.

DOES ALZHEIMER'S DISEASE RUN IN FAMILIES?

Some forms of Alzheimer's disease do run in families. Among these inherited forms, we know the most about the extremely rare type of Alzheimer's that begins as young as age forty or fifty. Less than one percent of all patients with Alzheimer's have this early-onset disease. Because many of these patients carry a mutation from birth, a blood test can detect the mutation before the disease begins.

The more common older-onset variety of the disease is usually not inherited. If one or more members of the family have the disease, it may be because Alzheimer's is common, not because the disease is in the genes. Even among identical twins, one twin may get the disease and the other may not. Except for the rare inherited form of Alzheimer's, genes are only one of several factors that determine whether you will get the disease. If you are concerned about inheriting Alzheimer's disease, you should raise this topic with your physician.

IS THERE ANYTHING I CAN DO IF ALZHEIMER'S DISEASE RUNS IN MY FAMILY?

The suggestion that Alzheimer's disease lies dormant in your body until late adulthood is frightening. Fortunately, only the few with early-onset Alzheimer's are doomed to get the disease solely because of their genetic makeup. More commonly, a particular gene will increase or decrease the risk of getting the disease. Risk is a concept we all deal with every day. For example, each day the weather report gives the chance, or probability, that it will rain. Some people carry umbrellas only if the risk is very high. Others carry umbrellas only when it is actually raining outside. And some take no chances and always carry umbrellas. Think of the umbrella as your worries: each of us has a different threshold before we take out the umbrella.

One gene that affects the risk of getting Alzheimer's disease is called ApoE. This gene comes in different types, called alleles. Type 4 increases the risk of getting the disease. Type 2 may decrease the risk. And type 3, which most people have, neither increases nor decreases the risk. Because people inherit genes from both parents, we each have two ApoE alleles. This is the way it works: half of the people with two type 3 ApoE alleles will get Alzheimer's disease by age eighty-five. This is the risk for most of us. If one allele is ApoE 4, the risk of getting Alzheimer's disease increases; if both alleles are ApoE 4, the risk increases even more.

Suppose you learn that your ApoE is type 4. Is there any way to reduce your risk of getting Alzheimer's disease? Right now we do not know how, but the search is on. More important, the actual increased risk conferred by ApoE 4 is quite small for any individual, and therefore knowing what type of ApoE you have is probably not worth the worry.

BESIDES GENETIC PREDISPOSITION, ARE THERE OTHER RISK FACTORS?

Of course the greatest risk for Alzheimer's disease is age. This is a disease to which the elderly are highly vulnerable. It is not, however, an inevitable consequence of aging. We all know of people who reach an advanced age without any cognitive impairment, including such highly accomplished people as Georgia O'Keeffe, Pablo Picasso, and George Burns. We still have much to learn about the ingredients of successful aging.

Women have a greater risk of getting Alzheimer's disease than men. Even taking into account the well-established fact that women live longer than men, women still get Alzheimer's disease slightly more often. Changes associated with aging in women, such as decreased estrogen, may be responsible, but a great deal more research is required to learn how hormonal changes affect the brain.

IS THERE ANYTHING THAT WE EAT THAT CAUSES ALZHEIMER'S DISEASE? HOW ABOUT ENVIRONMENTAL RISK FACTORS?

Nothing in the diet or in the environment has yet been identified as a cause of Alzheimer's disease. Some researchers have suggested aluminum or zinc exposure as a factor in getting the disease, but such possibilities have neither been substantiated nor widely accepted. At this point there is no scientific reason to suspect any dietary or environmental cause of the disease.

SHOULD AN ALZHEIMER'S PATIENT BE TOLD THE DIAGNOSIS?

Often when a patient comes to be evaluated for Alzheimer's disease, family members ask the doctor not to tell the patient if the diagnosis is confirmed. For families that suspect or know the diagnosis, deciding whether or not to tell the patient can be an agonizing decision. Families often try to hide the truth because they fear that the patient will be devastated. But when asked, most people say they would want to know. Most physicians, nurses, and ethicists believe that if patients are able to understand the diagnosis, they should be told. Even if their verbal communication is impaired, they may still be able to understand; patients often remain very expressive emotionally and capable of communicating their fears and wishes, even after their ability to use words is gone.

Telling a patient that he or she has cancer is important because decisions about treatment must be made. But Alzheimer's disease does not have an effective treatment. The most practical reason to inform is because the person may want to plan for a time when decision making is no longer possible. There is also a principle involved: the right to know is a matter of human dignity.

Surprisingly, Alzheimer's patients often appear indifferent to the diagnosis when they hear it. Sometimes they forget after they are told; sometimes they deny it. Facing the disease often seems more difficult for the family than for the patient, and it comes as a relief to the family that the word *Alzheimer's* can be spoken openly. But medicine is a field without absolutes, and there are patients for whom knowledge of the diagnosis can be terribly hurtful. Your doctor should recognize the sensitivity of this issue, and seek the best setting to discuss the implications of Alzheimer's disease with the patient.

HOW SHOULD THE CAREGIVER RESPOND TO THE ODD BEHAVIOR OF AN ALZHEIMER'S PATIENT?

If there is a single rule for getting along with a person who has Alzheimer's disease, it is cooperating with their views and wishes up to the point that no harm is done. I know a woman who took her mother to the grocery store in a nightgown, rather than force her to dress against her will. Caregivers may have to answer the same question over and over again. For instance, patients may know that they have an upcoming appointment, but they may not be able to remember when it is. Feeling anxious about getting there, they may ask repeatedly about the appointment even though it is still days away. The caregiver requires an extraordinary, at times superhuman, amount of patience, and some failures are natural.

Sometimes the caregiver has to intercede. The patient must be bathed regularly, even if he or she resists. Sometimes a patient's driving privileges may also have to be revoked. These practical necessities may create overwhelming frustration for Alzheimer's victims, who can resort to a catastrophic reaction, or "temper tantrum." Fortunately, these episodes pass quickly, often within a few minutes, and are forgotten; but in a brief bout of anger a patient can be very destructive. Because each person is different, you may need help from a nurse or social worker in dealing with these difficulties.

A Case: Tolerance of odd behavior

Three years after Mr. L's mother was diagnosed with Alzheimer's disease, he arranged for her to move in with his family. The only other alternative was a nursing home, because she was no longer independent. Soon some unexpected benefits resulted from this arrangement. They often went to the movies together, and even though Ms. L had almost no understanding of the movie, she seemed to enjoy the on-screen action and the family outing. She kept herself occupied by cleaning small specks of dirt from her clothes and often sat reading a book, which she also did not comprehend. Visibly enjoyable for her was the company of the family dog. On one occasion she tore up a twenty-dollar bill to feed to the dog. Her affection for animals extended to squirrels and even insects; feeding these creatures became part of her daily routine. Her family saw this period of the disease as a time toward the end of life in which to renew their sense of the kind of woman their mother was. They saw her as generous, as one who delights in all living things.

WHEN SHOULD A PERSON WITH ALZHEIMER'S STOP DRIVING?

Families often struggle with the issue of driving. Here are the facts. In general, Alzheimer's disease does negatively affect the patient's ability to drive. But each person is different and has to be individually evaluated. The diagnosis of Alzheimer's disease alone does not mean that a person should stop driving.

As the disease advances, the chance of an accident increases. Sometimes a good intermediate step is to limit the patient's driving to local destinations and to have them avoid highways. Eventually, and sometimes against great resistance, it may become necessary to prohibit all driving. If there is a disagreement about driving competence (and there often is), one solution is to have the person take a driving test. In fact, you and the patient can both take a driving test. If the patient fails, you can revoke driving privileges with more authority, and if the patient succeeds, you can allow driving with more peace of mind.

An automobile is a complex and potentially dangerous piece of machinery. Another dangerous piece of machinery to which many people have access is a gun. As with automobiles, families must impose restrictions on access to firearms when they suspect mental impairment in a loved one.

A Case: Driving was the issue

Ms. G came to see me along with her husband and son. I had already diagnosed her with Alzheimer's disease the previous year. Now she had gotten lost in a parking lot, after searching for her car. This terrifying experience prompted her son to inquire whether his mother should continue to drive. His question resulted in a very indignant response from Ms. G and her husband. He insisted that she drove well and that as long as he was with her, she should continue to drive. Clearly parents and son differed. Because I knew that Ms. G was moderately affected with Alzheimer's, I suspected that her driving might be impaired. I suggested that Ms. G should take a driving test to satisfy her son and me. In this case, the simple suggestion of a driving test was enough to convince Mr. G that he should take over more of the driving.

HOW CAN I MAKE THE HOME SAFE FOR AN ALZHEIMER'S PATIENT?

As the perceptions of a person with Alzheimer's disease dim, previously safe parts of the house can become dangerous. The patient's difficulty in distinguishing the hot-water tap from the cold may create the danger of scalding. It's best to prevent this problem by turning down the temperature of the hot-water heater. There are other common and sometimes unsuspected dangers. The patient may confuse artificial fruit with the real thing. The patient may leave the oven or range on, creating a fire hazard. He may lock himself in the bathroom and be unable to get out, which can be prevented by removing locks on bathroom doors. He may also wander outside, which can be minimized by installing complex locks on exterior doors. One family connected a motion detector to an alarm clock to detect wandering. Foot pads by the side of the bed can also be used to activate an alarm if the patient gets up at night.

Interpreting the meaning of sounds can also become difficult for the patient. A radio or TV in the next room may sound like strangers conversing in the house and can be frightening. Disconnecting remote speakers may be a partial solution. Screening out background sights and noises and paying attention to the matter at hand are abilities most of us take for granted, but those with Alzheimer's disease may have trouble directing or sustaining their attention.

Is there a cure?

As of this writing, Alzheimer's disease is incurable. As scientists learn more, piece by piece, about how the disease inflicts its ravages on the brain, optimism that a cure is possible is growing. Because we know the biochemical pathways that lead to the disease, we therefore have a foundation upon which a cure can be based. What no crystal ball can foretell is when an effective treatment will emerge. Unfortunately, the powerful desire for a cure can lead to a less than critical judgment about current treatments. As with any incurable disease, patients, families, and even medical professionals tend to grasp at all manner of passing treatments, whether folk remedies or medications that have not been proven effective.

If someone you love has Alzheimer's, it can be difficult to ignore anecdotal reports about remedies that were said to have helped a neighbor or a friend. Although keeping an open mind about new treatments can be useful, caution is the watchword. Sometimes unproven treatments only take advantage of the consumer's longing for a cure. It's the job of the physician, usually a neurologist, to keep informed about new treatments, and you should expect your doctor to provide you with such information.

ARE THERE ANY SYMPTOMS OF ALZHEIMER'S THAT CAN BE TREATED?

Although no cure is yet available for Alzheimer's, some of the symptoms of the disease can be treated. The most commonly treated symptom, agitation, affects seventy to ninety percent of patients with Alzheimer's disease at some point. Signs of agitation may include verbal and physical aggressiveness, irritability, disturbing hallucinations, wandering at night or outside the home, and restlessness. Major tranquilizers, such as haloperidol, are one hundred percent effective in controlling the symptoms of agitation. But these drugs often have side effects, such as drowsiness and muscular rigidity, which cause patients to appear as if they have Parkinson's disease. Physicians must use this medication in very low doses because the elderly are sensitive to medications; they must also periodically reevaluate the need for the medication because Alzheimer's disease is progressive and the patient's needs change.

Another category of medication sometimes used for symptomatic treatment of Alzheimer's disease is that of antidepressants. It can be difficult to tell if a demented patient is depressed; surprisingly, many patients at various stages of decline are not. On the other hand, some patients showed modest improvement after taking antidepressant medications, even if they did not appear depressed before taking the medication.

It is always best to avoid medications until they become necessary. Therefore, other approaches to helping patients with either agitation or depression should first be considered. Sometimes a reward system to reinforce good behavior is useful. A day care program may help with depression by providing a happier or healthier environment.

WHY DO UNPROVEN DRUGS SOMETIMES SEEM TO WORK?

Doctors can choose from a large catalog of medications when prescribing a drug. When no effective treatment is available, the temptation to choose a drug of unproven or marginal efficacy is great because physicians want to make every effort to cure the patient's ills. Thus, doctors may prescribe a medication even though there is insufficient evidence that the medication is effective. Such medications are usually very safe and may even be products that occur in nature, such as vitamin E and lecithin. An improvement detected during these "treatments" is called a placebo effect.

Placebo effects are actual improvements, though usually modest in degree. Scientists attribute the success of placebos to the power of will and belief, which gives each of us some measure of control over our minds and bodies. Nowhere is this phenomenon more obvious than among the practitioners of acupuncture in China, where the most important criterion for the use of acupuncture anesthesia before surgery is whether the patient believes in acupuncture. Sometimes just the hope or faith that improvement is possible has a therapeutic effect.

WHAT LIES AHEAD IN THE RESEARCH ARENA?

Scientists around the world are vigorously searching for medications that will help patients with Alzheimer's disease. As a result, many research centers offer experimental treatment programs in which volunteers serve as human subjects. Patients who participate in these trials are making a genuine contribution toward finding a cure. However, because so many drugs must be evaluated before a successful one is discovered, placing hopes in an experimental drug is a recipe for disappointment. Nevertheless, the staggering scientific advances over the past few years will certainly translate into a cure.

A final thought

With the sorrow and weariness that Alzheimer's disease brings, positive emotions, renewed possibilities, and even discoveries about the loved one and ourselves may also be experienced, as well as patience, tolerance, humor, and a capacity to shift priorities. Above all, there is love without hope of compensation or gratitude. If this small book can ease the trial of Alzheimer's disease to any extent, it has served its purpose.

As a close friend of mine wrote about her mother, afflicted with Alzheimer's: "Taking care of my mother has been an odd sort of blessing. It has allowed us to look in wonder at the true goodness of her character, to be awed by her kindness, and to witness every day how precious and delightful life is in all its forms, especially the form of my mother."

Resources

SELECTED ORGANIZATIONS THAT PROVIDE ASSISTANCE WITH ALZHEIMER'S DISEASE

Please note: Telephone numbers are supplied throughout; however, they may change.

Aging Network Services, 4400 East-West Highway, Suite 907, Bethesda, MD 20814. Telephone: 301-657-4329.

Alzheimer's Association, Alzheimer's Disease and Related Disorders Association Inc., 919 Michigan Ave., Suite 1000, Chicago, IL 60611-1676. Telephone: 800-272-3900. One of the most comprehensive sources of information, the Alzheimer's Association can also refer you to the Alzheimer's Association chapter nearest you. The Benjamin B. Green-Field National Alzheimer's Library and Resource Center has an extensive collection of printed materials and videotapes for caregivers, as well as a catalog that includes many free guides on specific topics.

Alzheimer's Association Safe Return Program (available from the Alzheimer's Association, above). The Safe Return Program offers information to help caregivers manage patients who wander, as well as identification bracelets and clothing labels, and it maintains a list of individuals with dementia who enroll. The program's services enable police, community agencies, and private citizens to rapidly identify any program enrollee. All local Alzheimer's Association chapters have Safe Return Program applications.

Alzheimer's Disease Education and Referral Center (ADEAR), P.O. Box 8250, Silver Spring, MD 20907-8250. Telephone: 800-438-4380. Mandated by Congress as a clearinghouse for information on Alzheimer's disease, ADEAR has a large database, a newsletter called *Connections*, and a World Wide Web home page. You may ask the ADEAR Center for a topical search (a list of materials on a specific subject).

American Association of Homes and Services for the Aging, 901 E St. NW, Suite 500, Washington DC 20004-2037. Telephone: 202-783-2242. Offers guides to housing options and long-term care.

American Association of Retired Persons, Program Resources, 601 E St. NW, Washington, DC 20049-0001. Telephone: 800-424-3410. Publishes free publications on long-term and home care and financial planning.

American Health Care Association, 1201 L St. NW, Washington, DC 20005-4014. Telephone: 202-842-4444. Offers free booklets on long-term care, including "Thinking about a Nursing Home."

American Massage Therapy Association, 820 Davis St., Suite 100, Evanston, IL 60201-4444. Telephone: 312-761-AMTA. Call for local recommendations. Massage can be very helpful for Alzheimer's patients.

Asociación Nacional Pro Personals Mayores (National Association for Hispanic Elderly), 3325 Wilshire Blvd., Suite 800, Los Angeles, CA 90010-1784. Telephone: 213-487-1922. Provides services, booklets, and referrals.

Assisted Living Facility Association of America, 9401 Lee Highway, Suite 402, Fairfax, VA 22031. Telephone: 703-691-8100. Offers a consumer checklist for evaluating facilities.

Choice in Dying, 200 Varick St., Suite 1001, New York, NY 10014-4810. Telephone: 212-366-5500. Offers free state-specific living will and durable power-of-attorney forms.

Eldercare Locator. Telephone: 800-677-1116. A nationwide telephone service that provides information about services offered by state and area agencies for families and patients with Alzheimer's disease.

Legal Services for the Elderly, 130 W. 42d St., 17th Floor, New York, NY 10036-7803. Telephone: 212-391-0120. Offers legal information as well as a resource list of free publications, including materials on social security insurance, Medigap, and veterans' entitlements.

National Academy of Elder Law Attorneys, Inc., 1604 N. Country Club Rd., Tucson, Arizona 85716-3195. Telephone: 602-881-4005. Offers help in finding attorneys who specialize in elder law. Call and ask for the Experience Registry. Laws regarding trusts, living wills, powers of attorney, and health care proxies vary greatly from state to state and frequently change.

National Association for Continence, P.O. Box 8310, Spartanburg, SC 29305-8310. Telephone: 800-BLADDER (252-3337). Clearinghouse of educational materials on continence.

National Association of Area Agencies on Aging, 1112 16th St. NW, Suite 100, Washington, DC 20036-4823. Telephone: 202-296-8130. Provides referrals to local agencies.

National Caucus and Center on Black Aged, 1424 K St. NW, Suite 500, Washington, DC 20005. Telephone: 202-637-8400. Offers referrals and written material.

National Council of Senior Citizens, 1331 F St. NW, Washington, DC 20004-1171. Telephone: 202-347-8800. Provides referrals to long-term care services, nursing homes, and alternatives.

National Council on the Aging, 409 3d St. SW, 2d Floor, Washington, DC 20024. Telephone: 202-479-1200. Offers free caregiving pamphlets, a booklet called "Guide to Choosing a Nursing Home," and local referrals.

National Hispanic Council on Aging, 2713 Ontario Rd. NW, Suite 200, Washington, DC 20009-2107. Telephone: 202-265-1288.

National Hospice Organization, 1901 N. Moore St., Suite 901, Arlington, VA 22209-1714. Telephone (Hospice HelpLine): 800-658-8898.

National Pacific/Asian Resource Center on Aging, Melbourne Tower, 1511 3d Ave., Suite 914, Seattle, WA 98101. Telephone: 206-624-1221.

Simon Foundation for Continence, P.O. Box 835, Wilmette, IL 60091. Telephone: 800-237-4666. Offers free information packets.

United Seniors Health Cooperative, 1331 H St. NW, Suite 500, Washington DC 20005-4706. Telephone: 202-393-6222. Offers free booklets on nursing-home and Medigap insurance, financial planning, and long-term care.

FURTHER READING

Alzheimer's Disease and Marriage. L. Wright. Medical University of South Carolina. 1993. 148 pp. Available from Sage Publications, Inc., 2455 Teller Rd., Newbury Park, CA 93120-2218. Telephone: 805-499-9774. This book discusses the effect of Alzheimer's disease on the marital relationship (sexual relations, household chores, commitment, companionship, and tension) and helps professional caregivers to assess the situation and intervene. Presents the perspectives of both the caregiver and spouse with Alzheimer's.

Alzheimer's Disease Mealtime Interventions. Lake County Health Department, Health Facilities Division, Waukegan, IL. 1993. 1 1/2-inch VHS videocassette (17:15 min), color. Includes manual, 56 pp. Available from Lake County Health Department, Health Facilities Division, 3012 Grand Ave., Waukegan, IL 60085. Telephone: 708-360-6733. This videotape and manual describe how environment and situations can confuse patients and disrupt eating. The videotape shows vignettes of effective and noneffective mealtime caregiving strategies, and the manual contains checklists of aspects of mealtime that can be used for evaluation and planning treatment for patients.

Hidden Treasures: Music and Memory Activities for People with Alzheimer's. C. Cordrey. Eldersong Publications, Inc. 1994. 106 pp. Available from Eldersong Publications, Inc., P.O. Box 74, Mount Airy, MD 21771-5260. Telephone: 301-829-0533. This manual shows professional and family caregivers how to use music to communicate with people with dementia. Describes how to develop a music program, sessions for patients with Alzheimer's disease, activities for seasons and holidays, and general music activities. Lists goals and step-by-step instructions for each activity described.

Preventing Caregiver Burnout. J. Sherman. Pathway Books. 1994. 77 pp. Available from Pathway Books, 700 Parkview Terrace, Golden Valley, MN 55416. Telephone: 612-377-1521. This book offers caregivers advice on recognizing warning signs of caregiver burden and preventing burnout. Reviews the stages and causes of burnout and describes strategies aimed at prevention. Causes of caregiver burnout include changing roles, unrealistic expectations or goals, lack of control, criticism from others, financial concerns, panic, grief, denial, overload, and isolation. Some ways to prevent caregiver burnout include positive thinking, humor, respite care, effective planning of case management, communication, and support.

The Thirty-Six-Hour Day. N.L. Mace and P.V. Rabins. Baltimore: Johns Hopkins University Press, 1991. Revised ed. 329 pp. Available from Warner Books, 1271 Avenue of the Americas, New York, NY 10020.

Understanding Alzheimer's Disease. M.K. Aronson, ed. Scribner's, 1988. 365 pp. Publication of the Alzheimer's Disease and Related Disorders Association.

Ethnic and Minority Issues

"AgeLines: Forgetfulness among American Indian and Alaska Native Elders." National Eldercare Institute on Long-Term Care and Alzheimer's Disease. 1994. 2 pp. Available from National Eldercare Institute on Long-Term Care and Alzheimer's Disease, Suncoast Gerontology Center, University of South Florida, Health Sciences Center, 12901 Bruce B. Downs Blvd., MDC Box 50, Tampa, FL 33612-4799. Telephone: 813-974-4355 or Fax: 813-974-4251. Single copy free. This fact sheet for Native Americans focuses on how to show respect and love for older relatives and deal with family members who are forgetful and confused due to dementia. Suggestions include remaining calm, reminiscing about the past, keeping the person safe, ensuring that the person eats properly and is healthy, overseeing caregivers taking care of themselves, and listening carefully to the person so that important communication is not missed.

"Boletín de la Edad Avanzada: Cuando Alguien Que Usted Conoce Sufrede la Enfermedad de Alzheimer" ("AgeLines: When Someone You Know Has Alzheimer's Disease"). National Eldercare Institute on Long-Term Care and Alzheimer's Disease. 1994. 2 pp. Available from National Eldercare Institute on Long-Term Care and Alzheimer's Disease, Suncoast Gerontology Center, University of South Florida, Health Sciences Center, 12901 Bruce B. Downs Blvd., MDC Box 50, Tampa, FL 33612-4799. Telephone: 813-974-4355 or Fax 813-974-4251. Single copy free. This fact sheet in Spanish describes how to interact with patients with Alzheimer's disease and how to support family caregivers. Outlines symptoms and behaviors of Alzheimer's and lists ways of preventing agitation and frustration. Also available in English.

"Boletín de la Edad Avanzada: Las Siete Señales de Alarma de la Enfermedad de Alzheimer" ("AgeLines: The Seven Warning Signs of Alzheimer's Disease"). National Eldercare Institute on Long-Term Care and Alzheimer's Disease.

1994. 2 pp. (Available from the address for "Boletín de la Edad Avanzada," above.)

Long-Term Care

Alzheimer Special Care in Nursing Homes: Is It Really Special? A Survey of Families and Professional Advocates. Alzheimer's Association, Public Policy Division. 1994. 63 pp. Available from Alzheimer's Association, Public Policy Division, 1319 F Street NW, Suite 710, Washington, DC 20004-1106. Telephone: 202-393-7737. University of Iowa researchers surveyed perceptions of professionals and family members about special care units (SCUs) for Alzheimer's disease patients. Professional advocates saw little difference between SCUs and traditional nursing homes. One-third of families said they are paying more for SCUs and are satisfied with the care. Most professionals favored rules governing the operation and evaluation of SCUs.

Choosing a Nursing Home for the Person with Intellectual Loss. E. Lincoln, ed. Published by the Burke Rehabilitation Hospital. 1980. 14 pp. Available from Alzheimer's Disease and Related Disorders Association, Inc., 919 Michigan Ave., Suite 1000, Chicago, IL 60611-1676; or from Burke Rehabilitation Hospital, Community Relations Dept., 785 Mamaroneck Ave., White Plains, NY 10605-2593. Telephone: 914-684-0203.

Residential Settings: An Examination of Alzheimer Issues. Alzheimer's Association, Patient and Family Services. 1994. 84 pp. Available from Alzheimer's Association, Patient and Family Services, 919 North Michigan Ave., Suite 1000, Chicago, IL 60611-1676. Telephone: 800-272-3900. A conference report on residential settings and issues affecting the development and maintenance of residential programs for Alzheimer's patients.

Patient Support

Early Stage Alzheimer's Patient Support Groups: Research, Practice, and Training Materials. R. Yale. Special Projects Press. 1994. 134 pp. Available from Robyn

Yale, 1067 Filbert St., Suite 100, San Francisco, CA 94133-2507. Telephone: 415-673-3881. A manual for the development and management of support groups for people in the early stages of Alzheimer's disease. Provides guidelines for leading and evaluating support groups.

Materials from Alzheimer's Disease Education and Referral Center (ADEAR)
When ordering materials from ADEAR, specify the publication number. Single copies are available free.

"Alzheimer's Disease and Related Dementias: Legal Issues in Care and Treatment, 1994." Publication Z-86. The Advisory Panel on Alzheimer's Disease issued this special report to Congress to focus attention on legal issues affecting people with Alzheimer's disease, their families, health care professionals, and society in general. The report describes the following areas of law as they influence people with Alzheimer's and their families:

- *autonomy and incapacity*
- *voluntary transfers of decision making (durable powers of attorney and trusts)*
- *involuntary transfers of decision making (guardianships and conservatorships)*
- *medical decision making (advance directives and refusals of medical treatment)*
- *ethics of treating in the absence of advance directives*
- *federal involvement in medical decision making*

"Caregiver Stress." Publication S-23

"Progress Report on Alzheimer's Disease, 1995." Publication Z-90. An annual report summarizing research and developments in the study of Alzheimer's disease.

"Q and A on Alzheimer's." Publication Z-06.

Computer-Based Resources
The Alzheimer List is an Internet discussion group for patients, professionals,

family caregivers, researchers, public policymakers, students, and anyone with an interest in Alzheimer's disease or related disorders. The service is intended to provide an opportunity to share questions, answers, suggestions, tips. Topics have included drug therapy, depression, wandering, nursing home placement, research reports, aggression, caregiver support, patient abuse. All you need is an E-mail address and a modem; access is free. The list is not for advertising or seeking remote diagnosis or treatment. To subscribe send the message *subscribe Alzheimer* to majordomo@wubois.wustl.edu, leaving the subject line blank.

It is also possible to view Alzheimer List discussions and other linked documents via the Alzheimer gopher site at http://gopher.adrc.wustl.edu:70 or the Alzheimer home page at http://www.biostat.wustl.edu/alzheimer. Some locales, such as the Cleveland area, have their own networks.

The Alzheimer's Disease Education and Referral Center (ADEAR) also has a World Wide Web site at http://www.alzheimers.org/adear.

Library of Congress Cataloging-in-Publication Data

Grollman, Earl A.
    When someone you love has Alzheimer's : the caregiver's journey /
Earl A. Grollman and Kenneth S. Kosik.
        p.   cm.
    Includes bibliographical references and index.
    ISBN 0-8070-2720-0 (cloth)
        1. Alzheimer's disease—Patients—Family relationships.
    2. Caregivers—Mental health. I. Kosik, K.S. (Kenneth S.), 1950–.
    II.   Title.
    RC523.2.G76   1996
    362.1'96831—dc20
                                                    96-15884